MW01601888

Forward:

There really IS a Little Swan Lake, maybe more than one. The Little Swan Lake in this story is located in West Central Illinois near the village of Avon. The lake was developed in the 1960's and in 2012 had over 200 homes located there. It is a pretty, peaceful lake used for fishing and boating by the members.

Leonard, also known as Aflak by the children, is a resident of Little Swan Lake. Most of us who live here check daily to make sure he is happily swimming about.

Special Thank You:

I have read many books to my daughters and grandsons over the years. They all enjoyed story time. So, to Deb, Michelle, Trevor and Owen ~~ this one's especially for you.

Thanks also goes to Keith, my constant supporter.

A special thank you to Tom & Linda Sawyer.

Copyright © 2012 by Judy Camp Rogers

LEONARD OF LITTLE SWAN LAKE

Written by

Judy Camp Rogers
Owen Torrance

Illustrations by Dorothy Ewald

Owen

Enjoy!
Judy Rogers

No one knows when a special duckling was hatched, but it was a few days before Easter. A young lady was shopping in a local farm store and saw the ducklings which were for sale. The ducklings were soft, fluffy yellow balls that were "cheeping" loudly.

She looked at them, then decided on the one she wanted. The duckling was paid for and carried to her car.

The duckling was wondering where it was going but the lady who bought it had a special home picked out. It was an Easter present for her parents, Mr. Tom and Miss Linda who live at Little Swan Lake.

The ride in the car seemed very long to the
duckling. His box was on the back seat of
the car and he could barely see out of the
window. He felt the bumps in the road and
could see the tree tops as they drove by.
Finally they arrived at Little Swan Lake.

The duckling's new home had a large grassy yard and a hill going down to the big lake ~~ it looked HUGE to the duckling. Mr. Tom had a nice cage to keep the duckling safe and a blue plastic pool with water in it for the duckling to swim in. Mr. Tom and Miss Linda fed the duckling bread crumbs and corn.

The duckling loved its' new home. There
were very tall trees with many birds
flying. Squirrels were looking for acorns
they had buried a few months earlier. The
duckling didn't see anything that looked
like him at all.

Mr. Tom and Miss Linda decided to call the duckling "Leonard." Leonard grew quickly and soon had beautiful white feathers and a bright orange beak. He now could "quack" instead of cheep. Leonard liked to explore the yard and one day Mr. Tom carried him down the hill to the lake. He gently placed Leonard in the water. The lake seemed much bigger than Leonard thought and he was a little scared.

After a short swim, Leonard went back to his cage and dreamed about swimming all over the lake.

Then came the day Leonard could go on the lake. He could swim anywhere but he did like to return to Mr. Tom for some corn and a safe place to sleep. Leonard looked everywhere for some ducks that could be his friend but there were none to be found. He started searching for friends.

He saw a big turtle sunning himself as he sat on some rocks. "Hi! My name is Leonard," he greeted. "Have you seen any ducks on the lake?"

"Hello, I am Timothy. I have seen brown ducks some days but none as pretty and white as you," the turtle said.

"I am looking for a friend," Leonard said.

"I will be your friend. You will find many friends here at Little Swan Lake," Timothy replied.

Leonard swam along the shore passing people fishing from the boats or dock and mowing their yards. He came to a snake swimming by and said "Hi! I am Leonard. Who are you?"

"Sammy" the snake hissed.

"Will you be my friend?" Leonard asked.

Not many people ask Sammy to be their friend so he was a bit surprised. He happily said "Yes, of course, I will be your friend."

Leonard would swim all day on the lake gathering friends. There were all kinds of birds including a huge eagle. There were hawks, black crows and a heron with very long legs. He liked the red cardinals and the yellow finches and the blue jays.

There were also furry critters around the lake. He met beavers, otter, fox, rabbits, squirrels, chipmunks and opossums. Some of them would go swimming and others just came for a drink of water. Most of them had lots of friends and weren't interested in a duck.

One day as he swam he was startled by
three deer that came to the water. They
stopped on the shore then one by one
jumped into the water and swam to the
other side. As they swam all Leonard could
see were their heads and ears.

There were many geese living at Little Swan Lake. Most of them were friendly to Leonard. He would swim with them or rest on the grassy lawns. In the spring they would hatch babies and the mommy and daddy geese didn't like to have Leonard around.

When the geese had rested they would start their loud honking noise, flap their wings and fly away. But when Leonard tried to leave with them he just could not fly. When he was hatched he had his wings clipped and try as hard as he could, he just couldn't fly.

In the fall and spring Little Swan Lake is a
stopping place for birds flying north or south.
These might be brown ducks, geese, white pelicans
and many other kinds. One winter some swans
stopped in and stayed for weeks. They were rather
"snooty" and didn't want to be friends.

Leonard had human friends who lived all around the lake. Children loved to have him swim by while they were swimming. Some called him "Aflak" and one boy would call "Lenny" from his dock. Leonard could see the humans looking for him and smiling.

He knew which person would have some
cracked corn or bread crumbs for him to
nibble on. Some of the food Leonard didn't
like very much. He didn't like dry crackers
or vegetables.

Leonard never forgets where his home is. He can swim back to Mr. Tom's house to find corn waiting for him. Miss Linda has some bread, too. Mr. Tom and Miss Linda sit on a bench watching the boats and Leonard likes to sit by their feet. He is very happy.

Leonard is a very lucky little duck and he knows it!